Animal Kingdom (Big Cats of the World): 2nd Grade Geography Series

Speedy Publishing LLC

40 E. Main St. #1156

Newark, DE 19711

www.speedypublishing.com

The term "Big cats" is commonly used in reference to large wild cats. All cats are carnivores and efficient apex predators.

The tiger is the largest of all big cats. The dark, vertical stripes that overlay the reddish orange color is one of the most noticeable characteristics of the tiger.

The cheetah
is the world's
fastest land
animal. The round
and black spots
on the cheetah
help them to
camouflage
when hunting.

The lion is the second-largest living cat after the tiger. Lions usually inhabit savannah and grasslands and will sometimes be found in forests.

The snow leopard is a large cat native to the mountain ranges of Central and South Asia. Its life span is usually about 15-18 years.

The jaguar is the third-largest cat and the largest in the Americas. They are solitary predators and are known to regulate the populations of prey species.

The cougar is also commonly known as the mountain lion. The cougar is an ambush predator and pursues a wide variety of prey.

The leopard
has relatively
short legs and a
long body with
a large skull.
Leopards can be
found in regions
of sub-Saharan
Africa, West
Asia, the Middle
East, South and
Southeast Asia
to Siberia.